D1568701

The Life of a
BEAN

Clare Hibbert

Raintree
Chicago, Illinois

© 2005 Raintree
Published by Raintree, a division of
Reed Elsevier, Inc.
Chicago, IL 60602
Customer Service 888-363-4266
Visit our website at www.raintreelibrary.com

For more information address the publisher:
Raintree, 100 N. LaSalle, Suite 1200, Chicago IL
60602

Printed and bound in China by the South China
Printing Company
08 07 06 05 04
10 9 8 7 6 5 4 3 2 1

Library of Congress Cataloging-in-Publication
Data

Hibbert, Clare, 1970-
   Life of a bean / Clare Hibbert.
      p. cm. -- (Life cycles)
   Includes bibliographical references (p.   ) and
index.
   ISBN 1-4109-0541-1 (lib. bdg. : hardcover)
   1. Beans--Life cycles--Juvenile literature. I. Title.
Series: Hibbert, Clare, 1970-   Life cycles.
   SB327.H53 2004
   635'.652--dc22
                              2004002734

Acknowledgments
The publishers would like to thank the following
for permission to reproduce photographs:
p. 4 Alamy Images; pp. 5, 14, 16 N.A.
Callow/NHPA; p. 8 Tudor Photography; pp. 9,
12, 17, 19, 22, 23, 26, 28 Holt Studios; p. 10 Dr.
Jeremy Burgess/Science Photo Library; p. 11 Adam
Hart Davis/ Science Photo Library; p. 13 Patrick
Johns/Corbis; pp. 15, 21 Stephen Dalton/NHPA;
p. 18, 24 Nature Picture Library; p. 20 Steve
Hopkin/Ardea; p. 25 Joel W. Rogers/Corbis; p. 27
D. Robert and Lorri Franz/Corbis; p. 29 Corbis.

Cover photograph of a bean, reproduced with
permission of Ecoscene.

The publishers would like to thank Janet Stott
for her assistance in the preparation of this book.

Every effort has been made to contact copyright
holders of any material reproduced in this book.
Any omissions will be rectified in subsequent
printings if notice is given to the publishers.

Contents

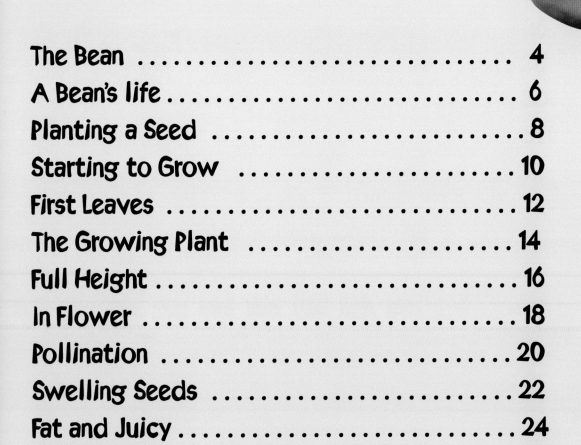

Any words appearing in bold, **like this,** are explained
in the Glossary.

The Bean

Beans are vegetables, which can be delicious to eat. There are many different kinds of beans. Beans are harvested to eat fresh, frozen, or canned. In some parts of the world they are roasted and salted like peanuts.

Beans grow inside long, fleshy pods.

Growing up

Just as you grow bigger year after year, the bean plant grows and changes, too. Beans grow in **seed** pods on bean plants. Beans are the seeds of a bean plant. It takes about four months for a bean plant to grow from a seed, put out flowers, produce its own seeds, or beans, and then die. The different stages of its life make up its **life cycle.**

Where in the world?

Beans have been grown as food for thousands of years. Today they are grown as crops all over the world. They prefer cool conditions, with rain and sunshine.

Many gardeners grow bean plants. They usually plant them in neat rows.

A Bean's Life

The **life cycle** of a bean begins with a **seed** planted in the ground in spring. Very soon the seed starts to grow, putting out **roots,** a **shoot,** and pairs of leaves. It will grow to be more than 3 feet (1 meter) tall.

Flowers and seeds

The bean plant produces sweet-smelling flowers. Each flower can swell to form a seed pod. Between four and eight little beans develop inside the pod. These seeds can be eaten, or planted to grow into new bean plants.

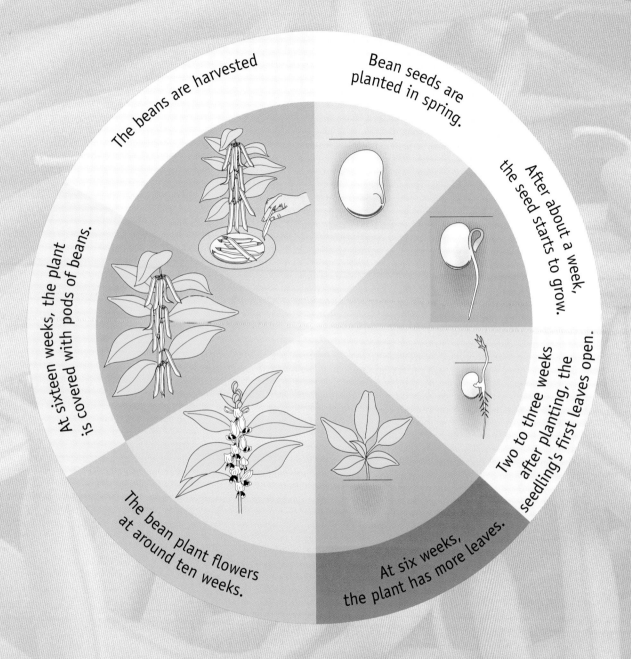

The beans are harvested

Bean seeds are planted in spring.

After about a week, the seed starts to grow.

Two to three weeks after planting, the seedling's first leaves open.

At six weeks, the plant has more leaves.

The bean plant flowers at around ten weeks.

At sixteen weeks, the plant is covered with pods of beans.

This diagram shows the life cycle of a bean, from seed to bean pod.

Planting a Seed

The bean **seed** is planted in spring. At this time of year the weather is warm, but not too hot. There are gentle spring rains to give the growing plant the water it needs.

Preparing the ground

A gardener digs into the ground using a fork. This makes the soil crumbly so that the plants' **roots** can easily push through it. The gardener also gets rid of any weeds that might crowd out the bean plants.

Beans are planted in a narrow line. Then they are covered over with soil and watered.

The gardener plants the beans about 1 inch (3 centimeters) below the surface, with about 6 inches (15 centimeters) between each seed so the plants will have space to grow. Then he or she waters the seeds. They need **moist** soil so that they can start to grow.

Fields of beans

Bean plants are not only grown by gardeners. Farmers grow whole fields of beans. They do not plant the seeds by hand, though. They use big machines called planters to do the job.

Farmers can attach a special planter to their tractor and use it to plant big fields of beans.

Starting to Grow

About a week after it is planted the bean **germinates,** or starts to grow. A **seed** needs **moisture** and warmth in order to germinate. A blanket of soil provides both. The warmth comes from the spring sunshine, which warms the soil. The water comes from the rain or from the gardener's watering can.

The bean seed puts out a long, white root. This stretches down into the soil to find water.

Root and shoot

The seed splits its skin, or husk, and pushes out a root. The root grows down into the soil. Its job is to suck up water for the plant from the ground.

Over the next week, the seed puts out a folded, leafy **shoot.** This pushes its way to the surface, toward the light.

This bean was planted about ten days ago. Its leafy shoot is heading for the surface.

Dried out

Not every bean germinates. Sometimes the conditions are not right. An example would be if there is not enough rain. Dry soil is no good for the bean plant. The seed needs a good soaking before it can germinate.

First Leaves

It is now two weeks since the bean **seed** was planted. Its shoot has broken through the surface of the soil. Its white stem has straightened out. The tiny leaves at the top of the stem are starting to open out.

Making food

Leaves make the food that the bean plant needs to grow. They do this by using gas, water, and light.

The shoot reaches the surface about two weeks after planting. It is a seedling.

The gas is carbon dioxide, which comes from the air. Each leaf has tiny holes that take in the carbon dioxide. The water comes from the soil and is taken in by the plant's **roots.** Light comes from the sun. Together these three ingredients make food for the plant. This process is called photosynthesis. It would not be possible without a substance in the leaves called **chlorophyll.** Chlorophyll makes the leaves look green.

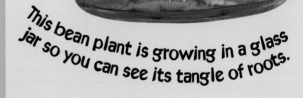

This bean plant is growing in a glass jar so you can see its tangle of roots.

Under the soil

By now, the root is almost 4 inches (10 centimeters) long. Shorter roots branch off from the sides. The roots take in water and **nutrients** from the soil. They also help to keep the plant steady so that it does not fall over.

The Growing Plant

During the next few weeks, the bean plant is busy putting out grayish-green leaves. By the time it is six weeks old, it has about eight leaves. The more leaves the plant has, the more food it can produce and the faster it can grow.

These young plants are about seven weeks old. They need to be watered if the weather is dry.

Bushy bean

Many types of beans grow on tall, thin vines. Many types wrap themselves around things as they grow. They need sticks to support them, otherwise they would blow over in the wind. Some bean plants are different. Their stem is thick and strong. The plant's bushy shape does not usually need any support.

Bean aphids

Sometimes the bean plant's stem comes under attack. Bean aphids are **insects** that suck plant juices from the stem. This weakens the whole plant. In bad cases, the plant might not grow strong enough to put out many flowers.

Bean aphids cover the plant's stem and suck the **sap**.

Full Height

Some types of bean plant may grow as tall as an adult person, while others may stop growing at around 12 inches (30 centimeters). Once it has reached its full height the plant stops making more leaves. It puts all its energy into producing flower **buds** instead.

Pest control

Not all insects are pests. Flies and ladybugs help the bean plant. They are **predators** that hunt and eat aphids. During its six-week life a ladybug can munch its way through nearly 2,500 aphids!

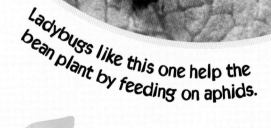

Ladybugs like this one help the bean plant by feeding on aphids.

Packed petals

The flower buds appear in tight groups at the base of the leaves. Each bud is protected by pale green **sepals.** These are like petals, but tougher. They protect the tightly packed flowers inside from insects that eat plants, such as aphids and blackflies.

These plants are about nine weeks old. The flower buds are just forming.

In Flower

Now the bean plant is about ten weeks old. Its flower **buds** are bursting open. Although bean plants are grown for their beans, their flowers are beautiful, and they smell good, too.

The bean plant's flowers are white with dark purple spots.

Male and female

Each flower has an important job to do. It will produce the **seeds,** which are also called beans. To do this, male and female flower parts will have to come together. These parts are in the middle of the flowers. The male parts are the **stamens.** The stamens carry grains of yellow **pollen.** The female part is called the **carpel.** It contains the flower's eggs, or **ovules.**

The male and female flower parts are hidden inside the petals.

Pollination

The flowers' color and scent attract honeybees and other **insects.** They visit the flowers to collect **pollen** for food, and to drink **nectar.** Nectar is a sugary liquid. The flower makes it to bring insects that will help it to produce **seeds.**

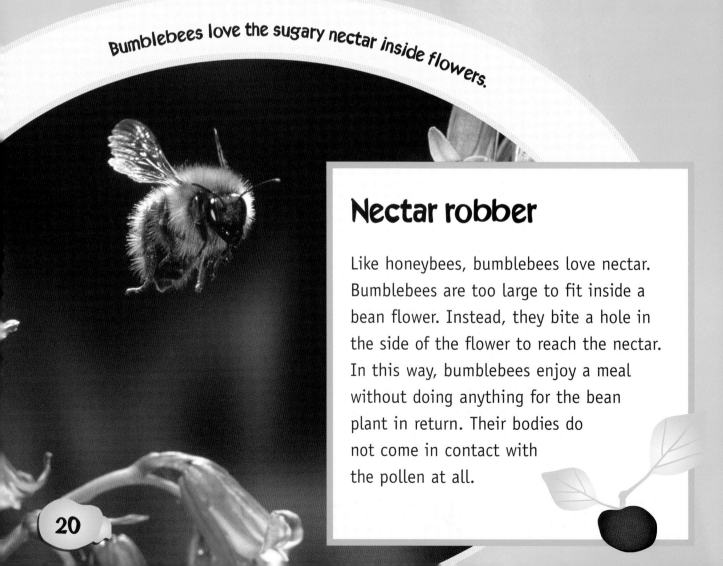

Bumblebees love the sugary nectar inside flowers.

Nectar robber

Like honeybees, bumblebees love nectar. Bumblebees are too large to fit inside a bean flower. Instead, they bite a hole in the side of the flower to reach the nectar. In this way, bumblebees enjoy a meal without doing anything for the bean plant in return. Their bodies do not come in contact with the pollen at all.

Grains of pollen stick to the honeybee's body as it gathers nectar from flowers.

Climbing in

To reach the nectar a honeybee has to wiggle to the center of the bean flower. As it does this, grains of pollen stick to its body. When the honeybee visits another flower the pollen rubs off onto that flower's female part. The pollen **fertilizes** the flower's **ovules** so that seeds can start to grow. This is called **pollination.**

Swelling Seeds

Once it has been **fertilized,** the flower's job is done. The plant does not need to attract pollinating **insects** any more. The petals lose their scent and blow off in the wind, but the stalk and **sepals** stay on the plant.

At the end of each bean pod, you can see the remains of the sepals that protected the flower.

Seed pods

The part of the stalk just under the sepals starts to swell. It is going to become a long **seed** pod. Each flower cluster produces between one and four pods. Inside each pod tiny seeds are starting to grow.

The pod is made mostly of water. If there is not much rain the gardener or farmer has to water the crop every day so that the pod can swell.

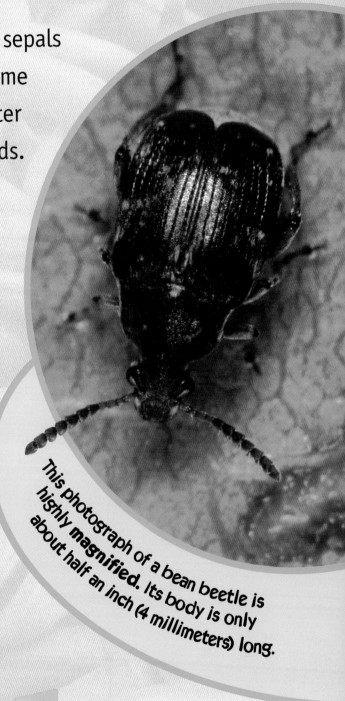

This photograph of a bean beetle is highly magnified. Its body is only about half an inch (4 millimeters) long.

Evil weevil

The bean weevil lays its eggs on the bean pods. Thirteen days later, tiny **larvae** hatch from the eggs. The larvae burrow into the pod and into the growing bean. These insect babies are tiny. Sometimes as many as five can share the same bean!

23

Fat and Juicy

During the next four weeks the bean pods grow bigger and bigger. Each one has a tough skin that protects the beans inside. The pod also has a soft, woolly lining that cushions the beans.

As the beans grow bigger, the pods begin to bulge.

Bean food

There are many pods, and each one contains between four and eight beans. Short, green stalks attach the beans to the pods. The stalk carries water and **nutrients** to the growing beans. The water and nutrients are collected from the soil by the plant's **roots.**

Not all gardeners want to share their plants. A scarecrow helps to keep the birds off the bean plants.

Birds and beans

Animals, especially birds, like to eat beans. Sometimes the bean passes right through the bird's body. It drops to the ground and might even grow the following spring. The movement of **seeds** away from the parent plants is called seed dispersal.

Bean Harvest

The bean plant is now twenty weeks old. You can see the bulging shapes of the beans inside each pod. Each pod is speckled with black and may be up to 8 inches (20 centimeters) long. The beans are ready to be harvested. They have not quite finished growing, but they are sweeter to eat now.

These speckled pods are ready to pick. Inside, the beans are plump and tasty.

Reaping and threshing

Gardeners pick their beans by hand. Farmers use big machines called reapers that cut down the whole plant. Then they use another machine, called a thresher, to pull out the beans. The rest of the plant does not go to waste. As it rots, it puts all of its **nutrients** back into the soil.

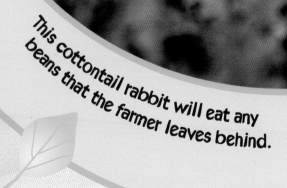

This cottontail rabbit will eat any beans that the farmer leaves behind.

Bean snacks

Some pods fall on the ground and split open. Hungry animals, such as field mice, rats, and rabbits, sniff them out and enjoy a bean feast.

The Dying Plant

Once all the bean pods have finished growing, the plant starts to die. The stem stops carrying water to the leaves so they wither and turn yellow. Next the stem dries out until it snaps like an old twig.

Now the bean plant has no leaves. Any pods that were not picked turn almost black.

New life

By the time fall comes around, the plant is dead. Any pods left on the plant turn dark brown and become hard. The beans inside these pods can be stored to plant next spring. Beans that have fallen to the ground might even survive the winter. Each could grow into a whole new bean plant, and the **life cycle** could begin all over again.

Beans are full of nutrients. They make a great meal for hungry cattle.

Animal feed

Some types of bean are grown for animals to eat. Horses and cattle can eat the rest of the plant, not just the bean.

Find Out for Yourself

The best way to find out more about the life cycle of a bean is to grow some. You can grow beans in a pot on a balcony, in your garden, or in your school garden if you have one. You can also find out more by reading books about beans, and by looking for information on the Internet.

Books to read
Charman, Andrew. *I Wonder Why Trees Have Leaves and Other Questions about Plants*. New York City: Kingfisher Books, 2003.

Morgan, Sally. *Life Cycles: Sunflowers and Other Plants*. London: Belitha Press, 2001.

Using the Internet
Explore the Internet to find out more about beans and other plants. Websites can change, so if some of the links below no longer work, don't worry. Use a search engine, such as www.yahooligans.com, and type in keywords such as "bean," "pollination," and "life cycle."

Websites

www.brainpop.com/science/plantsandanimals/pollination
Watch the mini cartoon showing how flowers produce seeds.
www.raw-connections.com/garden/index.htm
A great site of gardening tips, whether you want to grow flowers or vegetables.

Glossary

bud tightly packed shoot that may open out into a leaf or flower

carpel female part of a flower. It is made up of the stigma, style, and ovary.

fertilize when pollen joins with an ovule to create the beginnings of a new living thing

germinate to grow from a seed, putting out a shoot and root

insect animal that, as an adult, has three body parts, three pairs of legs, and, usually, two pairs of wings

larva young insect that looks nothing like its parent

life cycle all the different stages in the life of a living thing

magnify make something look much larger than its actual size

moist slightly wet

nectar sugary food that flowers produce to attract pollinating insects, such as bees

nutrient substance in food that a plant or animal needs to grow properly

ovule female cell, or egg, that can grow into a seed when it has joined together with pollen

pollen powdery grains that contain the male cells of a flower

pollination when male pollen from one flower is carried to the female part of another flower

predator animal that hunts other animals and eats them for food

root part of a plant that pushes down into the soil. Its jobs are to suck up water and to steady the plant.

sap plant juices

seed small package produced by a plant that contains the beginnings of a new plant inside it

sepal outer petal that protects a flower when it is still a bud

shoot stem like growth that comes out of a seed once it has germinated. The shoot pushes up through the soil toward the light, where it will be able to put out leaves and develop into a stem.

stamen male part of the flower.

Index

OCT 29 '94